The Official
Manchester City
Football Club
Annual
2006

Written by
David Clayton

A Grange Publication

© 2005. Published by Grange Communications Ltd., Edinburgh, under licence from Manchester City Football Club. Printed in the EU.

Designed by Steven James.

With special thanks to Manchester City photographer, Edward Garvey

ISBN 1-902704-93-2

£6.99

Shaun Wright-Phillips v Charlton Athletic 28/08/04

More fool the defence that gives Shaun space within shooting distance of goal – and that's exactly what Charlton's defenders did in this match. From fully 30 yards out and with no challenge, Shaun let fly with a swerving shot that fooled Dean Keiley in goal and flew into the roof of the net for his first goal of the season.

Robbie Fowler v Fulham 14/08/04

This was the Blues' first goal of the 2004/05 season and perhaps should have been the winner. An awkward cross came towards Robbie Fowler who cleverly hooked the ball over his shoulder and past Edwin van der Sar. A stunning volley and typical of Fowler's ability to score out of nothing.

Claudio Reyna v Tottenham 19/03/05

After missing most of the season with injury, Claudio Reyna returned to the team to replace the injured Shaun Wright-Phillips. The USA skipper was in inspirational form on the right of midfield and when Robbie Fowler played the ball into his path he hit a stunning half-volley in off the post for his first goal of the season.

7 Shaun Wright-Phillips v Aston Villa 27/11/05

Yet another cracker to add to his huge collection of wonder-strikes. As the ball was laid into Shaun's path he let fly with a bullet shot that was rising all the time to leave the goalkeeper with no chance.

8 Shaun Wright-Phillips v Southampton 01/01/05

What a way to start the New Year! Picking up the ball 40 yards out Shaun span his marker cleverly, shimmied one way before sending a low shot from 30 yards out that hit the inside of the post before nestling in the back of the net.

9 Kiki Musampa v Aston Villa 07/05/05

A great move that ended with a stunning strike. As City worked the ball down the right, Jon Macken cleverly dummied a pass that left Kiki Musampa with a clear sight of goal. From the edge of the Villa area, the Dutch winger sent a banana shot past the keeper and high into the net to give City a crucial 2-0 lead.

10 Shaun Wright-Phillips v Barnsley 21/09/04

The Barnsley defence were torn apart during an amazing first half that saw City score five goals. One of them was a SWP special. He ran down the left before drawing the goalkeeper off his line and sending a beautifully weighted chip over his body and into the net. Pure class!

Contents

Welcome

Welcome to the third Manchester City Annual! We hope you enjoy looking back over last season and ahead to what looks like an exciting campaign for 2005/6. City just missed out on Europe last year after a late surge of form and will be looking to continue pushing for a European spot this season.

Stuart Pearce was confirmed as the new manager just before the last home game of 2004/5 and he will be looking for City to stay amongst the top six, where they belong, but this time from the word go! Everton and Bolton have proved that it's not just a select group of sides that can qualify for European competition and City will be doing their very best to ensure the top clubs from across the continent will be visiting the magnificent City of Manchester Stadium next year.

We have introduced a few new features in this year's Annual, including a special Junior Blues section and Moonchester and Moonbeam's own pages – well, they did insist! As usual, there are lots of quizzes scattered throughout so get your thinking caps on and remember – no cheating by looking at the answers page at the back! So enjoy the Annual and keep cheering the Blues on – the best team in the land – and with your support - all the world!

KING RICHARD!

Player of the Year: Richard Dunne

For the first time in quite a while, there were several strong contenders for City's Player of the Year 2005. As ever, Shaun Wright-Phillips was among the favourites after cracking in 11 spectacular goals during last season (including one for England). David James hardly put a foot (or a hand!) wrong and played in all 38 Premiership games and both Sylvain Distin and Robbie Fowler had been consistently good all season. Joey Barton was another possibility, but when the votes were counted it was defender Richard Dunne who won the award – his first such honour after finishing runner-up to Shaun Wright-Phillips last year.

It was no more than Dunne deserved after such high levels of consistency throughout the campaign – and he even managed to score two goals! Dunne, not renowned for scoring in the opposition's net (he has been cruelly credited with a couple of own goals in recent seasons), has become a greater threat from set pieces since Stuart Pearce became manager. In fact, he was unlucky not to have another thanks to referee Graham Poll ruling out a cracker at West Brom.

But Dunne would argue that his job, first and foremost, is to stop the other team scoring and his partnership with Sylvain Distin did an admirable job in that department, becoming one of the best defensive pairings in the Premiership. He also won his place back in the Republic of Ireland side, after being strangely overlooked for several months by the new manager. If there's been a better Irish defender than Dunne over the past 18 months, then good luck to him – but we know there hasn't been anyone better than him, don't we? Injury kept him out of the last few games last season but by then he'd already done enough to win the coveted award of best player.

THE BOSS!

Stuart Pearce became City's new manager just a few days before the end of the 2004/5 season. It's fair to say that when he took over from Kevin Keegan, many people thought it would be only until the end of the season but Pearce thought differently from day one.

He had been on City's coaching staff since the summer of 2002 after deciding to hang his boots up for the final time. He played just one, inspirational season for the Blues, helping them easily win the old First Division (now The Championship) and on his final appearance had a chance to score his 100th career goal when City were awarded a last-minute penalty against Portsmouth.

With the Maine Road crowd urging him on, he ran up, hit the ball true – but wide of the target! The wry smile on his face would be repeated exactly three years later in May 2005 when a similar situation would end City's season.

Kevin Keegan had been so impressed with Pearce, he then offered the former

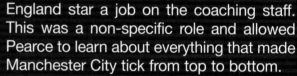

England star a job on the coaching staff. This was a non-specific role and allowed Pearce to learn about everything that made Manchester City tick from top to bottom.

He assisted training with the first team, reserves and paid special attention to the blossoming Academy at Platt Lane. He sat in with Keegan on contract negotiations and new signings and scouted around the UK and Europe when required. In short, by the time he was promoted to joint first team coach at the beginning of the 2004/5 season, there wasn't much about the club he didn't know!

Many people credited City's improved defensive organisation to Pearce that season and he publicly stated that he had his eye on Keegan's job when the current boss came to end of his contract at the end of the 2005/6 campaign. But pressure grew on Keegan to leave earlier because of a run of disappointing results.

With 10 games left it was vital they didn't just fall away and have a flat end. A terrible home defeat by Bolton was the end of the road for Keegan. The team looked to be lacking in motivation and Keegan looked as though even he was losing his enthusiasm. The manager agreed with the chairman it was time to let somebody else have a go and Keegan recommended Pearce be given the opportunity – the board decided that was the right thing to do.

With just nine games left, Pearce had to convince the players, fans and board that he could take the club forward. He had limited experience in managing a team but his standing in the game was second-to-none. He was a born winner – but could he transfer his personal qualities into management?

His first game was at Tottenham and despite a 2-1 defeat, it was clear that the team has been given a major boost and the Blues were desperately unlucky to lose. Was it a fluke? The next game at Charlton saw City play their best football in a long time and again, they should have come away with all three points and but for better finishing, they would have.

Pearce knew the pressure was building for that first win. Next up were Liverpool and with 90 minutes played, the score was 0-0 – was his luck ever going to change? The answer was yes, as Kiki Musampa volleyed home a winner with seconds left.

The fans loved it and a draw at Fulham, win against Birmingham and another point at Blackburn proved that the players wanted to play for Pearce. Victories over Portsmouth and Aston Villa also meant that the Blues could – unbelievably take the final UEFA Cup spot with a win over Middlesbrough in the final game.

The fans demanded Pearce be given the job permanently and with just three days to go before the final match of the season, Chairman John Wardle announced Pearce was the new manager of Manchester City.

On a dramatic final day, with scores level against Middlesbrough, City were awarded a penalty in injury time… but Robbie Fowler couldn't complete the fairytale start for Pearce and his kick was saved and the manager was left with the same wry smile he'd had when he himself missed with the last shot of his career.

It was a dramatic and wonderful end to the season for the City fans that hailed Stuart Pearce as their hero. Many believe he will lead the club to great things in coming years – let's hope so!

So close!

The 2004/5 season began with hopes of a much better campaign than the previous one. City had finished in 16th spot, just six points above relegated Leicester and things had to improve. The opening game against Fulham gave them the chance for a perfect start and when Robbie Fowler spectacularly put City ahead in the first half, the Blues seemed on their way to three points. But Collins John equalised and Fulham almost scored a shock winner late on and the crowd of 44,026 went home largely disappointed.

Danny Mills and Ben Thatcher were the only new signings and the £100,000 spent in transfer dealings in the summer was the lowest amount invested in a long, long time. Clearly, Kevin Keegan had to get the best out of the players he already had but defeats at Liverpool and Birmingham left the Blues second bottom with three games played.

They needed a win against Charlton Athletic in game four – and got it! The 4-0 saw the first goals of the season for Shaun Wright-Phillips and Trevor Sinclair as well as two more for Nicolas Anelka. City leapt up to tenth in the table and things seemed much better. Next at the City of Manchester Stadium were Everton – the team beaten 5-1 for the final game of the previous campaign by the Blues. The capacity crowd expected more of the same.

But Everton were a different proposition this time around and Tim Cahill's headed winner (he was sent off for the celebration) was hugely disappointing. But two more Anelka goals gave City their first away win at Crystal Palace and a 7-1 win over Barnsley in the Carling Cup just three days later meant the next game against Arsenal could be approached with confidence.

It was a tight game but Ashley Cole's one-two and fine finish gave the Premiership titleholders a 1-0 win. A point at Southampton was followed by the visit of league leaders Chelsea who were still unbeaten – could City end their run? The answer was yes! With 16 minutes gone the Blues were awarded a controversial penalty and Anelka stepped up to score what would prove to be the winner – and Chelsea's only league defeat of the season.

It was a great platform to build on but despite fighting all the way at Newcastle, Craig Bellamy fired in a late winner to give the Geordies a 4-3 win. Arsenal returned to win again, this time 2-1 in the Carling Cup and a 1-1 draw with bottom club Norwich saw more points thrown away.

The first Manchester derby of the season was at Old Trafford and few expected City to gain anything from the game. But a magnificent defensive display with David James and Stephen Jordan outstanding earned the Blues a creditable 0-0 draw, but yet again they followed up a great result with a flat performance, this time against basement club Blackburn, with a 1-1 home draw.

The inability to string a couple of wins together was affecting any hopes of European football but the 3-1 win at Portsmouth was followed by a 2-0 win at home to Aston Villa and at last City moved

beyond tenth place into ninth. Nobody knew what was coming next and as Middlesbrough raced into a 3-0 lead in the next game, it looked like a heavy defeat was on the cards. But Fowler and Bradley Wright-Phillips almost inspired an unlikely point but the Blues ran out of time, losing 3-2.

Then an impressive Tottenham side won 1-0 at the City of Manchester Stadium – and that was followed by a great win 1-0 at Bolton and Joey Barton's first Premiership goal of the season. At this stage, City were averaging four points from every three games and if that continued, a total of around 52 points would at least guarantee there would be no concerns of relegation.

The defence looked solid and Shaun Wright-Phillips, David James, Richard Dunne and Sylvain Distin had all been consistently excellent. But the infuriating inconsistency struck again as City ended the year with a 2-1 loss at Everton and a 1-1 home draw with then-bottom West Brom – that meant that each time the Blues had played the team at the bottom so far, they had drawn 1-1 on home soil.

At least the New Year began more brightly with a 2-1 win over Southampton and a terrific draw at Arsenal, where Shaun Wright-Phillips scored a magnificent goal. That was also the last game for Nicolas Anelka who would soon leave for Turkish side Fenerbahce. Anelka seemed determined to move on but it was a big blow for the thousands of young City fans who loved the French striker.

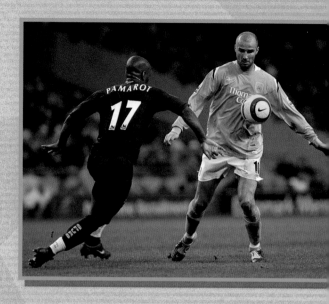

Maybe an FA Cup run would give the fans hope of silverware and when City were paired with Oldham, it seemed the chances of progress were good – but the Blues had saved their worst display so far for the cup and lost 1-0 to a team two divisions below them.

Keegan needed his side to banish the memory of Oldham with a great display against Crystal Palace – and he got it. City played sparkling football and won 3-1 to move back up to ninth in the table, but again, when the chance to progress presented itself, as it did with an away trip to West Brom, disappointment followed. Albion, still bottom, deservedly won 2-0 in a game best remembered for Richard Dunne's spectacular – but disallowed free-kick.

A point at home to Newcastle, in which new loan signing Kiki Musampa made his debut, and a super 0-0 draw away to Chelsea, where David James made a breathtaking last-minute save, was followed by a 2-0 loss to Manchester United. It seemed another defeat would follow at Norwich where City were soon 2-0 down, but goals from Antoine Sibierski and Robbie Fowler brought the scores level and Fowler scored again a minute from time

to secure a pleasing 3-2 win – and Fowler's 150th Premiership goal – a record bettered only by Alan Shearer and Andy Cole.

Another win against Bolton would boost European hopes but City were poor and lost 1-0. Few realised that it would be Kevin Keegan's last game in charge. Stuart Pearce took over and despite losing his first game at Spurs, he inspired the team to play bright, attacking football with the team performing as though their lives depended on it.

Successive away draws at Charlton, Fulham and Blackburn were mixed with three successive home wins against Liverpool, Birmingham and Portsmouth, earning Pearce the manager of the month award for April. With two games left, City needed maximum points and results to

go their way in other matches. The win at Aston Villa meant victory over Middlesbrough and Spurs winning by less than a two-goal margin and City were in Europe.

It was an incredible end to the season and a 2-1 win at Villa set up what was in effect a cup final against Boro with the winner claiming the final spot in the UEFA Cup. With a fantastic atmosphere and a full house for that final game and the announcement Pearce had been given the job on a permanent basis, City almost did what had seemed impossible just two months before, but had to settle for a 1-1 draw after Fowler missed a last minute penalty.

The Blues finished in eight place, unbeaten in eight games – their best finish to a season and highest placing ever in the Premiership.

With a host of talented youngsters such as Lee Croft, Stephen Jordan, Nedum Onuoha, Bradley Wright-Phillips and Willo Flood all playing their part last season, Stuart Pearce – and the City supporters – will be hoping for more of the same and even greater success this season!

2004 - 2005 Quiz

Q1. Who was the only player to have played every minute of every Premiership game last season?

Q2. Who was the first player to be sent off last season and can you name the other two players to receive their marching orders?

Q3. Which team did Nicolas Anelka play against in his last appearance for City and what was the significance of the date?

Q4. Who did Lee Croft make his debut against?

Q5. Which team did Bradley Wright-Phillips score his first Premiership goal against?

Q6. Out of the following list, who was NOT born in London: Shaun Wright-Phillips, Bradley Wright-Phillips, Stuart Pearce, Ben Thatcher or Trevor Sinclair?

Q7. Three young City players represented England together in a game for the first time last season – who were they and what age group was it at?

Q8. What did the top three-placed Premiership clubs share in common when they played City on their own grounds?

Q9. Who was the youngest and who was the oldest player to play for City last season and what ages were they?

Q10. City were awarded six penalties last season and missed just one – who scored them?

2004/2005 SEASON RESULTS

Home / Away

DATE	VERSUS	SCORE	ATTENDANCE	POS	SCORERS
Aug 14	Fulham	1-1	44,026	-	Fowler
Aug 21	Liverpool	1-2	42,831	16	Anelka
Aug 24	Birmingham	0-1	28,551	19	
Aug 28	Charlton	4-0	43,593	10	Anelka 2, Sinclair, SW-P
Sep 11	Everton	0-1	47,006	13	
Sep 18	Crystal Palace	2-1	25,052	10	Anelka 2, (1 pen)
Sep 21	Barnsley (CC3)	7-1	19,578	-	Macken 2, Sibierski 2, SW-P, Barton, Flood
Sep 25	Arsenal	0-1	47,015	13	
Oct 2	Southampton	0-0	28,605	13	
Oct 16	Chelsea	1-0	45,047	10	Anelka (pen)
Oct 24	Newcastle	3-4	52,316	13	Fowler (pen), SW-P 2
Oct 27	Arsenal (CC4)	1-2	21,708	-	Fowler
Nov 1	Norwich	1-1	42,803	12	Flood
Nov 7	Man United	0-0	67,863	13	
Nov 13	Blackburn	1-1	45,504	12	Sibierski
Nov 20	Portsmouth	3-1	20,101	11	Sibierski, Bosvelt, SW-P
Nov 27	Aston Villa	2-0	44,530	9	Macken, SW-P
Dec 6	Middlesbrough	2-3	29,787	11	Fowler, BW-P
Dec 11	Tottenham	0-1	45,805	12	
Dec 18	Bolton W	1-0	27,274	10	Barton
Dec 26	Everton	1-2	40,530	11	Fowler
Dec 28	West Brom	1-1	47,177	12	Anelka
Jan 1	Southampton	2-1	42,895	10	Bosvelt, SW-P
Jan 4	Arsenal	0-0	38,086	9	
Jan 8	Oldham (FAC4)	0-1	13,171	-	
Jan 15	Crystal Palace	3-1	44,010	9	Fowler, SW-P 2
Jan 22	West Brom	0-2	25,348	9	
Feb 2	Newcastle	1-1	45,752	10	Fowler (pen)
Feb 6	Chelsea	0-0	42,093	10	
Feb 13	Man United	0-2	47,111	11	
Feb 28	Norwich	3-2	24,302	10	Sibierski, Fowler 2
Mar 7	Bolton W	0-1	43,050	12	
Mar 19	Tottenham	1-2	35,681	12	Reyna
Apr 2	Charlton	2-2	26,436	12	Fowler, Hreidarsson (og)
Apr 9	Liverpool	1-0	47,203	11	Musampa
Apr 16	Fulham	1-1	21,796	11	Reyna
Apr 20	Birmingham	3-0	42,453	11	Dunne, Sibierski (pen), Taylor (og)
Apr 23	Blackburn	0-0	24,646	10	
Apr 30	Portsmouth	2-0	46,454	9	Distin, Fowler
May 7	Aston Villa	2-1	39,645	8	SW-P, Musampa
May 15	Middlesbrough	1-1	47,221	8	Musampa

2004/2005 PLAYER STATS

CITY CAREER STATS

	League Apps.	Gls.	Cups Apps.	Gls.	League Apps.	Gls.	Cups Apps.	Gls.
David James	38	-	1	-	55	-	1	-
Danny Mills	29(3)	-	3	-	29(3)	-	3	-
Richard Dunne	35	2	1	-	152(5)	2	21(1)	-
Sylvain Distin	38	1	3	-	110	3	17	1
Ben Thatcher	17(1)	-	3	-	17(1)	-	3	-
Stephen Jordan	19	-	-(2)	-	19(3)	-	-(2)	-
Nedum Onuoha	11(6)	-	1	-	11(6)	-	1	-
Claudio Reyna	16(1)	2	-	-	35(5)	3	6(2)	-
Joey Barton	28(3)	1	2	1	59(7)	3	9(4)	1
Shaun Wright-Phillips	33(1)	10	3	1	130(23)	26	21(7)	5
Trevor Sinclair	2(2)	1	1	-	22(11)	2	9(1)	1
Antoine Sibierski	34(1)	4	3	2	52(16)	9	7(3)	4
Kiki Musampa	14	3	-	-	14	3	-	-
Jon Macken	16(7)	1	2	2	27(24)	7	4(4)	5
Robbie Fowler	28(4)	10	1	1	63(13)	19	11	4
Bradley Wright-Phillips	-(14)	1	1(2)	-	-(14)	1	1(2)	-
Lee Croft	-(7)	-	-	-	-(7)	-	-	-
Willo Flood	4(5)	1	2(1)	1	4(5)	1	2(1)	1
Jonathan D'Laryea	-	-	1	-	-	-	1	-
Christian Negouai	-(1)	-	-(1)	-	2(4)	1	2(2)	1
Jihai Sun	4(2)	-	1	-	60(14)	3	13	1
Nicky Weaver	-(1)	-	-	-	145(2)	-	29	-
David Sommeil	1	-	-(1)	-	33	2	7(1)	1
Steve McManaman*	5(8)	-	-(1)	-	Released May 05			
Nicolas Anelka**	18(1)	7	-	-	To Fenerbahce Jan 05			
Ronal Waterreus	-	-	2	-	To Rangers Jan 05			
Paul Bosvelt	28	2	2	-	To Heerenveen May 05			

Barclaycard Premiership Final Table 2004/2005

		P	HOME					AWAY					PTS	
			W	D	L	F	A	W	D	L	F	A		
1	Chelsea	38	14	5	0	35	6	15	3	1	37	09	95	57
2	Arsenal	38	13	5	1	54	19	12	3	4	33	17	83	51
3	Man United	38	12	6	1	31	12	10	5	4	27	14	77	32
4	Everton	38	12	2	5	24	15	6	5	8	21	31	61	-1
5	Liverpool	38	12	4	3	31	15	5	3	11	21	26	58	11
6	Bolton	38	9	5	5	25	18	7	5	7	24	26	58	5
7	Middlesbrough	38	9	6	4	29	19	5	7	7	24	27	55	7
8	Man City	38	8	6	5	24	14	5	7	7	23	25	52	8
9	Tottenham	38	9	5	5	36	22	5	5	9	11	19	52	6
10	Aston Villa	38	8	6	5	26	17	4	5	10	19	35	47	-7
11	Charlton	38	8	4	7	29	29	4	6	9	13	29	46	-16
12	Birmingham	38	8	6	5	24	15	3	6	10	16	31	45	-6
13	Fulham	38	8	4	7	29	26	4	4	11	23	34	44	-8
14	Newcastle	38	7	7	5	25	25	3	7	9	22	32	44	-10
15	Blackburn	38	5	8	6	21	22	4	7	8	11	21	42	-11
16	Portsmouth	38	8	4	7	30	26	2	5	12	13	33	39	-16
17	West Brom	38	5	8	6	17	24	1	8	10	19	37	34	-25
18	Crystal Palace	38	6	5	8	21	19	1	7	11	20	43	33	-21
19	Norwich	38	7	5	7	29	32	0	7	12	13	45	33	-35
20	Southampton	38	5	9	5	30	30	1	5	13	15	36	32	-21

So you want to be
a Mascot . . . ?

Becoming an official MCFC Mascot, home or away, is every young City fan's dream . . . but remember . . . only Junior Blues are Mascots.

If, like every City fan, your dream is to represent Manchester City as their official Mascot, then first and foremost you MUST become a Junior Blue. Once a member . . . this is the way to do it.

Home mascots . . .

. . . are selected by competition only and must be aged between 5 & 12 years old. These competitions are found mostly in the bi-monthly Junior Blues News that all Junior Blues automatically receive. Club sponsors and local radio stations also run the occasional competition. If you are lucky enough to win, City then provide you with four match tickets, the kit of your choice, a special City goody bag and most importantly, the day of a lifetime!!

Away mascots . . .

. . . once again all applicants must be aged between 5 & 12. If you fit that category then simply write to the Junior Blues office at the City of Manchester Stadium, stating which game/games you would like to be considered for. These letters are placed on an away mascot file and drawn at random approximately one month before each fixture. Away mascots are also drawn at our regular Junior Blues events, but please note whilst we provide the appropriate kit, the remaining cost i.e. travel and tickets are the responsibility of the parents and this should be taken into consideration before applying. We automatically have four tickets on hold for you to purchase at the MCFC Ticket Store should your application be successful.

So if you're not a Junior Blue, what are you waiting for?!

THE PLAYERS ON TRIAL!

These are the clubs that the City players first had trials with:

Danny Mills – Norwich City

Danny played for the team he supported as a boy from the age of 11 – even though they rejected him as a 10-year-old - and remained with Norwich until he later transferred to Charlton Athletic.

Lee Croft – Crewe Alexandra

Wigan-born Lee Croft began life with Crewe before trying out his luck with City. Once he'd made his mind up to sign for the Blues he was approached by Everton, Manchester United and the club he supported – Liverpool. But fortunately, he had set his mind on being a City player.

Nedum Onuoha – City

Born and bred a Blue, when City and Manchester United showed interest in signing the young defender there was only one club he wanted to sign for and they didn't wear red shirts!

Richard Dunne – Nottingham Forest

Richard had trials with Nottingham Forest and he is another youngster they let slip through their net. Everton then took him on where he remained for several years before signing for City.

Ben Thatcher - Southampton

Ben's dad is a Southampton fan and he eventually had a trial with them but things didn't work out and Millwall signed him on instead. He stayed there until Wimbledon bought him and later moved on to Spurs and Leicester before joining the Blues.

David James – Tottenham

David was on trial for Spurs when Watford visited for a match. He ended up with a bad back he was beaten so many times but Watford still liked what they'd seen and offered him a trial at Vicarage Road where he eventually signed professional forms.

FAVOURITE AWAY GROUNDS

We all know that home is where the heart is and the City of Manchester Stadium is the players' favourite ground of all, but what about when City play away? Which is their favourite destination? Below we reveal all . . .

David James: Kenilworth Road, home of Luton Town

Possible reason: David started out at Watford; deadly rivals of Luton and his first game there must have created quite an impression.

Robbie Fowler: Anfield, home of Liverpool

Possible reason: Robbie spent most of his career at Anfield and was adored by the Liverpool fans who even nicknamed him 'God'!

Willo Flood: Anfield, home of Liverpool

Possible reason: We can't work this one out, unless Willo was a boyhood Liverpool fan!

Danny Mills: Elland Road, home of Leeds United

Possible reason: Danny enjoyed a successful spell at Leeds so he obviously has happy memories of Elland Road.

Nedum Onouha: Riverside Stadium, home of Middlesbrough

Possible reason: Not sure about this – we can't work out why any City player would enjoy playing at a stadium we have lost so many times! Maybe Nedum was having a joke!

Ben Thatcher: Millennium Stadium, home to Wales

Possible reason: Ben is a Welsh international and the atmosphere inside the Millennium Stadium for the national matches can be fantastic.

City Crossword

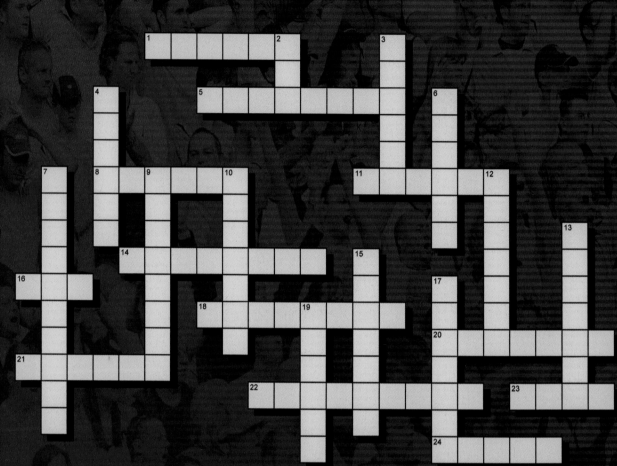

Questions Across:

01 Mikkel Bischoff went on loan twice to the same club last season – who was it? *(6)*

05 Team City scored seven goals against who in the cup last season *(8)*

08 First name of City player born in Toxteth *(6)*

11 Stephen, the Warrington-born defender *(6)*

14 Went to Oldham on loan for a short spell *(3,5)*

16 First name of City's only Welsh international *(3)*

18 The mascot who wears lipstick! *(8)*

20 Captain America's first name? *(7)*

21 Surname of the player who signed for Crystal Palace in the summer *(6)*

22 Which team did Stuart Pearce take charge against? *(9)*

23 First name of City's No.24 *(4)*

24 Nationality of Kiki *(5)*

Questions Down:

02 This City player sounds hot to touch *(3)*

03 Stuart Pearce's nickname *(6)*

04 Which Spanish city did Kiki Musampa arrive from? *(6)*

06 The chairman's surname *(6)*

07 Club Claudio Reyna joined City from *(10)*

09 Song all City fans sing *(4,4)*

10 Who was the first club to complete a league double over City last season? *(7)*

12 Birth country of Nedum *(7)*

13 Which country was former City player Andrei Kanchelskis born in? *(7)*

15 First name of the reserves' top scorer *(7)*

17 First name of City's player of the year *(7)*

19 Kevin Keegan left City after playing which club? *(6)*

Top Ten GOALS of the Season

1 Shaun Wright-Phillips v Aston Villa 07/05/05

Picking up the ball on the right, Shaun cut inside and shrugged off a couple of challenges before heading for the Villa box. He then dropped his shoulder and darted past another defender before firing a low drive past Thomas Sorensen for a wonderful solo goal.

2 Shaun Wright-Phillips v Arsenal 04/01/05

Shaun scored a fantastic goal at the ground where his dad Ian is still a legend. Picking up the ball 30 yards out from goal, he cut his foot across the ball as he sent in a powerful shot that curled into the top left-hand corner for an unforgettable goal. He sank to his knees as his team-mates mobbed him.

3 Kiki Musampa v Liverpool 09/04/05

With just seconds remaining and the game seemingly heading for a 0-0 draw, substitute Lee Croft picked up the ball near the halfway line and played it inside to Bradley Wright-Phillips. Bradley moved forward and then slipped the ball back to Croft who looked up to see Kiki Musampa free on the edge of the box. The cross was perfect and Musmapa's volley exquisite to give the Blues a last-minute winner.

DAVID JAMES

David James, who joined the Blues from West Ham in January 2004, is continuing City's proud history of great goalkeepers. The England custodian arrived as David Seaman retired and has been a rock at the back ever since. His communication skills are second to none and he is a great organiser who, along with Richard Dunne and Sylvain Distin in particular, helped make City's defence one of the meanest in the Premiership last season. In the three home and three away games against Chelsea, Arsenal and Manchester United, James conceded just four goals in

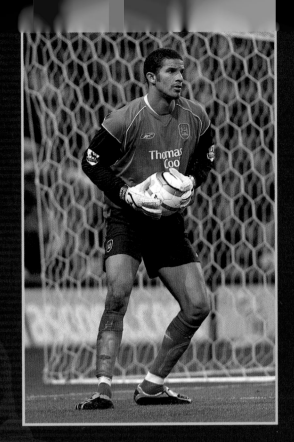

total. He kept 11 clean sheets during the campaign and made several inspirational saves along the way, though none better than the one at Stamford Bridge.

With the score locked at 0-0 and the game deep into injury time, the ball fell to Frank Lampard who let fly with a venomous drive from around 12 yards. The ball seemed destined for the bottom corner before James arched down to his right to push the ball around the post for a corner. It was an incredible save that James reckons is his best ever, as do many others who were amazed at his athleticism.

In the summer he was back in goal for England – he lost his place to Tottenham's Paul Robinson for much of the season for the national team. But Robinson's injury meant James, who Sven-Goran Erickson claimed has been totally professional whilst being on the bench for his country, reclaimed the jersey for the games against USA and Colombia. He will hope to keep his place and looks certain to travel as part of the squad to the 2006 World Cup in Germany.

City fans also reckon he's one of the best keepers of recent times – and they're right!

10 Facts About
Robbie Fowler

1. Name: Robert Bernard Fowler.

2. Born: Toxteth, April 9, 1975.

3. Team supported as a boy: Everton.

4. Favourite stadium: Anfield.

5. Robbie has played for England 26 times and scored 7 goals.

6. Honours: FA Cup Winner (2001), League Cup winner (1995, 2001), UEFA Cup Winner (2001) – all with Liverpool PFA Young Player of the Year 1994/95.

7. Scored quickest hat trick in Premiership history against Arsenal on August 28, 1994 – just 4 minutes 32 seconds!

8. Has scored 12 hat-tricks in professional career – 11 for Liverpool, 1 for Leeds.

9. Robbie scored his 150th Premiership goal against Norwich City making him third in the all-time list behind Alan Shearer and Andy Cole.

10. Squad numbers: 9, 23 (Liverpool) 8 (Leeds, Manchester City) 7, 27 (Manchester City).

Spot the Ball

Silhouettes

Can you guess who the two players are below?

WHERE IN THE WORLD?

New Jersey, USA **4**

Dublin, Ireland **8**

Lille, France **2**

Bagnolet, France **6**

Nigeria **9**

1
KIKI MUSAMPA

2
ANTOINE SIBIERSKI

3
JIHAI SUN

4
CLAUDIO REYNA

5
GEERT DE VLIEGER

There was a time when City players were mainly English with a few Irish, Scottish and Welsh players thrown in. Nowadays, the Premiership is a global industry and the Blues' squad of 2005/6 hails from many different countries and environments. Below is a world map showing exactly where on the planet some of the players have come from to play their football in Manchester.

7 Copenhagen, Denmark

5 Dendermonde, Belgium

Dalian, China 3

1 Kinshasa, Democratic Republic of Congo

6 SYLVAIN DISTIN

7 MIKKEL BISCHOFF

8 RICHARD DUNNE

9 NEDUM ONUOHA

YOUNG PLAYER OF THE YEAR

Nedum Onuoha

With such an exciting crop of young talent progressing through to City's first team in the past 12 months, choosing a winner for the Young Player of the Year 2005 was never going to be easy. There were several strong candidates including Bradley Wright-Phillips, Lee Croft and Stephen Jordan, all of who made an impact on the senior team at some point during the 2004/5 season.

But one name stood out more than most – Nedum Onuoha. It's easy to forget that he made his City debut aged just 17 when City played Arsenal in the Carling Cup and that he was still appearing for the Under-18s in the FA Youth Cup. The powerfully-built defender was then given the job of keeping Thierry Henry quiet when the Blues travelled to Arsenal in the league and he had an outstanding game during an impressive 1-1 draw. He then played in fits and starts before Stuart Pearce took over as manager and made him a first team regular. He also won his first England Under-20 cap and scored on his debut! Not a bad start for the youngster who penned a new deal towards the end of last season, which will see him become an integral part of the City defence. He has played most of his games at right-back, but his natural position is centre-back, and it is there that the club believe he will eventually end up playing on a regular basis.

For the young lad from Miles Platting, it has been a dream season and thanks to crowning a memorable year with the coveted Young Player award, one that the former school's sprint champion will never forget.

UPCOMING YOUNGSTERS 2005 - 2006

Micah Richards

A fast and powerfully built midfielder, Richards was voted Most Promising Young Player by City fans for 2005. Maturing all the time and tipped to have a bright future at the Club, Richards also has an eye for goal and bagged 13 goals in 25 appearances for the Under-18s and broke into the reserve team towards the end of last season. Can also play as centre-half.

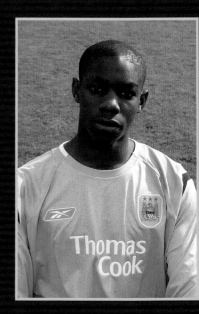

Ishmael Miller

At six feet four inches, Ishmael Miller is a daunting prospect for any defender. The Manchester-born striker has pace and sledgehammer shot that saw him score 20 goals in 29 starts for the Under-18s. He added seven in six starts for the reserves before grabbing the winner in the Manchester Senior Cup final against Manchester United. Expect to see him around the first team squad this season.

Stephen Ireland

Skilful and able to deliver neat weighted passes. Stephen Ireland's style is easy-on-the-eye and he became a regular fixture in the reserves last season after impressing for the Under-18s. With the departures of Steve McManaman and Paul Bosvelt at the end of last season, Ireland will be hoping to push his claims forward for the currently vacant role of playmaker.

Danny Warrender

Tough and uncompromising, Manchester-born Danny Warrender is an old-fashioned full-back who learned his trade at the Academy along with a host of other talented up-and-coming youngsters. His progress during 2004/05 was such that he was promoted from the Under-19s to the reserves and ended the campaign as second string captain. He also is a boyhood City fan who travels home and away to support the club whenever he can. He signed a new two-year deal in the summer of 2005 and will be hoping to see some senior action at some point this season.

Kasper Schmeichel

There is no need to introduce Kasper Schmeichel, son of former City goalkeeper Peter. The young Dane played for the reserves and the Under-18s last season and has already been on the bench for a Manchester derby! He still has much to learn but has the talent to go all the way.

Manchester City Football Club

MOONCHESTER

M.C.F.C.
Superbia In Proelio

MOONBEAM

GOOD GAME!
October 16, 2004
City 1 Chelsea 0

Chelsea were top of the table and progressing well in all competitions when they travelled to one of their traditionally lucky away fixtures – Manchester City. Chelsea had won many of the clashes between the clubs over the past 20 years and though most of their away wins came at Maine Road, they won on their first visit to the City of Manchester Stadium by 1-0, despite being outplayed for much of that game.

City knew they had to be at their best for this game and Chelsea, with nine wins and a draw in the last 10 meetings against the Blues in the Premiership, were still unbeaten under Jose Mourinho.

Both teams tested each other early on but it was City who got the first break when Nicolas Anelka tangled with Paulo Ferreira around the edge of the box – the referee decided it had been inside the penalty area and awarded a penalty. The Chelsea players complained but either way it had been a professional foul and Ferreira should have been sent off, but escaped an early bath. Anelka coolly stepped up to stroke home his sixth of the season and give City a priceless lead with just 11 minutes gone. It was only the second goal Chelsea had conceded all season!

With Chelsea having only managed eight goals in eight games, City knew they had a real chance of defending their lead successfully. But Chelsea were far from finished and began to dominate as the game wore on. Frank Lampard went close a few times and David James made at least three excellent saves. Sylvain Distin and Richard Dunne were fantastic at the back. City also lost Jihai Sun with a nasty knee injury but despite a simple late chance for Eidur Gudjohnsen, City held their nerve to record a famous win.

They'd ended the jinx, became the first team to beat Chelsea and, as it turned out, would remain the only club to beat the Londoners all season. Quite an achievement!

KIKI MUSAMPA

Moonchester's GUESS WHO?

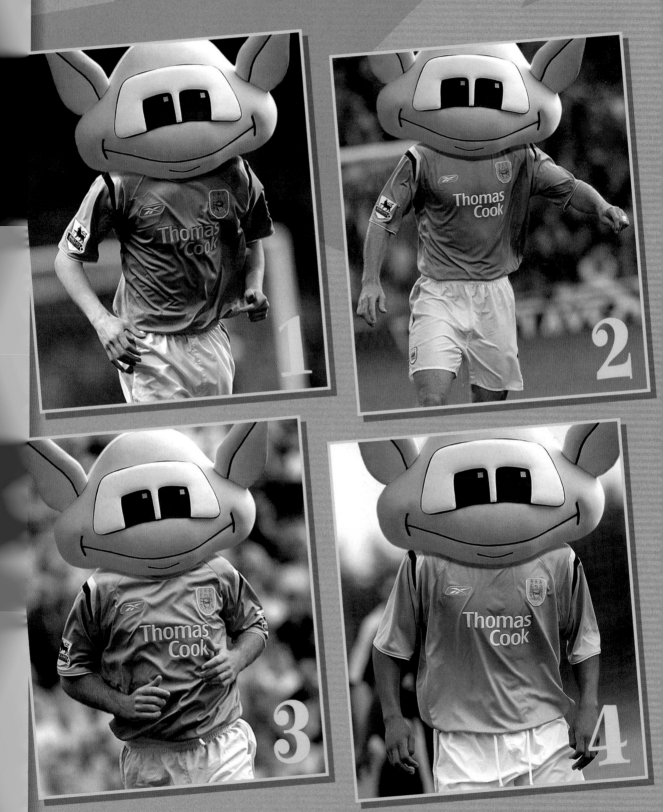

Can you guess which players are hiding under Moonchester's Head?

MANCHESTER CITY
Museum and Stadium Tour

Experience Manchester City with this exciting and interactive exhibition tracing City's prestigious heritage in a never to be forgotten day at the City of Manchester Stadium!

Be the next John Motson and commentate on glorious City goals! Relive favourite moments on the Video Jukebox. See the collection of City memorabilia covering every aspect of the Club's story.

Take a behind the scenes tour of the City of Manchester Stadium, including the players tunnel, dug outs and one of the executive lounges. See where the action really happens by visiting places that are strictly off-limits on matchdays – except for the players!

While enjoying your City Experience take a break at the City Social Cafe for a light snack or something more substantial, and visit the CityStore.

All in all, it's a day to remember.

Opening Times
All visits must be pre-booked. Call 0870 062 1894 to book.

Admission

Adults: £7.50
Concessions: £4.50
(includes disabled, children
under-16, over-65s)

Price includes City Experience
and Stadium Tour.

The Manchester City Experience and City Social Cafe are located above the CityStore at ReebokCity.

PLAYER PROFILES 2005 - 2006

An inspired signing from West Ham United, David James was one of the best buys former manager Kevin Keegan made during his tenure and his form since joining City has been fantastic. Commanding in the box, James has been in the form of his life since becoming a City player and is one of the main reasons the defence was so solid last season.

Made the Premiership save of the season – and probably a career best stop – when keeping an injury time shot from England team-mate Frank Lampard out at Chelsea and also played up front against Middlesbrough!

DAVID JAMES

Belgian international Geert de Vlieger must count himself as the unluckiest player of last season after injuring himself in a pre-season friendly at Wolves and being ruled out of the campaign.

He then suffered a setback during his rehabilitation that set him back several months and then, after finally being declared fit, injured himself in training near to the end of the 2004/5 campaign. Will be praying for better luck this year!

GEERT DE VLIEGER

City's longest serving player, Nick Weaver has been at the club for eight years and will be determined to see first team action this season after battling back from a series of morale crushing blows that stretch back for almost three years.

Weaver's courage should not be underestimated and most who have suffered similar injuries have never played again. The popular Sheffield-born goalkeeper will be on stand-by for David James and will likely be challenging Geert de Vlieger for the No.2 spot this season.

NICK WEAVER

A solid, experienced defender who can play in the middle or full-back in the back four, David Sommeil's first team opportunities were limited to just two appearances last season and the form of the defence as a unit means he will find it tough to break into the starting line-up this season.

Will be hoping to challenge for the role of centre half or full-back should any injuries or suspensions occur from those currently ahead of him in the queue.

DAVID SOMMEIL

Danny Mills signed from Leeds United last summer after spending a season on loan at Middlesbrough.

The experienced full-back was part of a tight-knit back four for most of last season but the emergence of young Nedum Onuoha saw him edged out of the side for the latter part of the campaign.

Can play centre-back as well and has a wealth of international experience to fall back on after his numerous appearances for England.

DANNY MILLS

Welsh international Ben Thatcher only managed to play in half of the games in 2004/5 due to various injuries that sidelined him for twice for two-month periods. Since then he has largely shared the left-back role with Stephen Jordan.

He seemed to be set for a move to Fulham until the deal broke down at the eleventh hour and now seems determined to re-establish himself in the Blues' defence.

BEN THATCHER

One of last season's success stories, Stephen Jordan seemed to be set for Peterborough United in the 2004 close season but decided to stay at the club he'd already spent 14 years with and give it one last go.

When Ben Thatcher was injured at the end of last October, Jordan was handed his chance in the first team and he performed so well that even when Thatcher was declared fit, he kept his place. Signed a new two-year deal during the summer.

STEPH JORDA

Arguably the success story of last season, Nedum Onuoha jumped from the Academy Under-18s into the first team in almost one fell swoop. The Manchester schools' sprint champion captained the Under-18s in the FA Youth Cup for the last time at Wolverhampton Wanderers before breaking into the first team on a regular basis when Stuart Pearce took over as manager.

He was rewarded with a new contract last April and showed his versatility when covering at centre-half (his favoured position) for Richard Dunne during the last two games of the season.

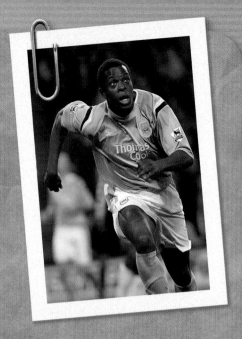

NEDUM ONUOHA

The City captain lead from the front all season during 2004/5 and grew into the captaincy more with each game. After admitting that initially wearing the armband affected his game the previous year he decided to just concentrate on doing things his way last season and was outstanding throughout in defence with Richard Dunne where the Blues earned a reputation as a tough nut to crack. He even chipped in with a rare goal and hopes to add more since a greater emphasis has been placed on set-piece situations since Stuart Pearce took over. He should also earn international recognition for France this season.

SYLVAIN DISTIN

City's Player of the Year for 2005, Richard Dunne was outstanding from start to finish and perhaps second only to John Terry for the honour of best centre-back in the Premiership. Dunne has always been dependable but his partnership with Distin was one of the main factors behind City's success last season and he also won back a place in the Ireland squad after mystifyingly being overlooked for several games. It's hard to imagine there was a better Irish defender but now he seems to be back in favour and must be a strong contender to represent his country in Germany should Ireland qualify for the World Cup finals.

RICHARD DUNNE

Now in his fifth season with the Blues, Chinese superstar Jihai Sun suffered a crippling knee injury against Chelsea in October 2004, ruling him out of the remainder of the campaign.

He had been in excellent form up to that point but despite the injury he was handed a new deal in the summer and should be raring to go during the 2005/6 campaign.

Versatile and whole-hearted, Jihai has been badly missed and his return to fitness will be a bonus to manager Stuart Pearce as City once again challenge for a UEFA Cup spot.

JIHAI SUN

Loaned from Atletico Madrid towards the end of last season, Kiki Musampa settled in well to the City team that made a late surge for Europe.

He had to adjust to the pace of the Premiership but once he did provided much needed balance down the left-hand flank and chipped in with a couple of crucial goals against Liverpool, Aston Villa and Middlesbrough.

City extended the loan for another year in time for the new season and he will be a useful addition to the squad.

KIKI MUSAMPA

Made one appearance last season against Arsenal and will be looking to push on again this season.

The nippy midfielder is yet another graduate of the Blues' Academy and his twin brother Nathan will also be hoping to impress Stuart Pearce in what is a crucial season for both players.

JONATHAN D'LARYEA

Impressed on his first few outings last season and will be hoping to push for more starts this campaign.

The young Ireland winger has pace and trickery and will benefit from adding a bit more muscle to his frame during the summer months to help him cope with the more physical side of life in the Premiership.

Scored a couple of goals and will be a good asset to the squad this season.

WILLO FLOOD

Wigan-born winger Lee Croft had to go on loan to Oldham to show what he could do at first team level and he returned with what then-manager Kevin Keegan described as a "spring in his step".

His five-minute cameo debut performance for City against Bolton proved he could cut it at Premiership level and his part in the winning goal against Liverpool for his second appearance earned him an army of new admirers among the City fans.

A dashing and direct right-winger, the club expect big things of Croft in 2005/6.

LEE CROFT

Looking more and more likely to earn full international honours before long, Joey Barton has made himself indispensable in the City first team.

Shedding his reputation for needless bookings and rash challenges, the Huyton-born ball-winner has physically filled out and matured into a fine player whose energy and effervescence has made him a big crowd favourite. Tipped as a future City captain, Barton could well force his way into Sven-Goran Eriksson's World Cup plans if he continues to blossom this season.

JOEY BARTON

Trevor Sinclair will be hoping to put a disastrous season behind him and return fully fit to challenge for a first team spot after almost a year on the sidelines with injury.

The midfielder has not enjoyed the best of luck since signing for his boyhood team and knows things can only get better.

The former England international will be keen to show what he is capable of and make up for lost time when he gets his chance again this season.

TREVOR SINCLAIR

Returned from a lengthy absence last season to play his part in the impressive end of season form the team showed as they climbed the Premiership table.

The skilful American international's neat play and clever passing added a new dimension to the Blues' midfield and he even managed to fill the boots of Shaun Wright-Phillips for a few weeks during the England midfielder's enforced absence. Will shoulder much of the team's creativity in the coming season and will skipper the USA team if they qualify for the 2006 World Cup in Germany.

CLAUDIO REYNA

The French attacking midfielder missed only two games and was asked to fill a multitude of roles within the team last season, but did so without complaint and with aptitude.

Skilful on the ground and good in the air, he will be disappointed not have scored more times for City but will always be a danger in the opposition's box.

ANTOINE SIBIERSKI

Earned the tag of super-sub after more than 15 appearances from the bench last term and will be eager to start more games this season.

A hugely promising striker who has plenty of tricks in his locker and a poacher's instinct for goal, Bradley has been prolific for the reserve side for the past two seasons and will be waiting for his chance to show what he can do at first team level after impressing the fans on his brief appearances to date.

Played for the England Under-20s in Toulon last summer and acquitted himself well.

BRADLEY WRIGHT-PHILLIPS

M.C.F.C.

Superbia In Proelio

Andrew Cole

Born in Nottingham in October 1971, Andrew Cole began his professional career at Arsenal as a teenager but, despite a loan spell with Fulham, he never broke into the Gunners' first team and in March 1992 he joined Bristol City for £500,000.

It was at Ashton Gate that the young striker really caught the eye of the top clubs' scouts, scoring 20 goals in 41 appearances for the Robins. But despite his impact, Bristol were not in a position to refuse a £1.75 million offer from Newcastle United and after just a year in the south west, Cole was off to St James' Park, where he would soon become something of a phenomenon.

In just 70 appearances for the Toon, Cole scored an incredible 55 goals and almost helped Kevin Keegan's side to the league title in the process. The team that pipped Newcastle, Manchester United, were so impressed with Cole that they stole him away for £6m in January 1995 – a move that caused anger and dismay among the Geordie faithful.

For Cole, however, it was the beginning of an amazing period of success and he spent seven years at Old Trafford, scoring 93 goals in 161 starts – he'd now bagged 168 goals in just 272 appearances in his career – a record that quite rightly placed him among the Premiership's all-time greats.

He moved to Blackburn in December 2001 for £7m and became a popular figure at Ewood Park but was in a team that struggled against relegation and he moved on again, this time to Fulham, where last season he scored 13 times in 39 starts. Second only behind Alan Shearer in the Premiership's all—time leading goalscorers, Cole began his City career with a debut goal against Everton in the 2005 Premier League Asia Cup in Thailand. It looks like he will continue his remarkable scoring record in a light blue shirt from now on!

Darius Vassell

It was as a prolific scorer for the Aston Villa youth team that Darius Vassell first caught the eye of the manager at Aston Villa. He scored an incredible 39 goals during the 1996/97 season and made his first team debut just two years later, coming on as a sub against Middlesbrough. It took a while for the jet-heeled forward to make his mark in the first team, however, and he often had to come off the bench to show what he was capable of. But in season 2001/02, he really arrived in the Premiership, scoring 16 times and forging a formidable partnership with Juan Pablo Angel.

In February of that season, he was given his England debut against Holland and Vassell scored a wonderful overhead kick to celebrate the start of his international career and his progress was such that he not only made the 2002 World Cup squad, he started the opening game in Japan.

Vassell had a fruitful 2002/03 and again was part of the England squad for a major tournament when he made four sub appearances during Euro 2004. Sadly for Darius, he missed a crucial penalty in the quarter-final shoot-out with Portugal and the sight of holding his head on the turf afterwards was an image few will forget.

Whether that miss affected his confidence or not is unclear, but many felt he needed a change of surroundings to kick-start his career again and when the offer to play for City came along, he jumped at the chance.

Now City has a proven Premiership striker with 14 England caps at a very reasonable price. If he can re-discover his best form and progress yet further for the Blues, he may well be on the plane to Germany in 2006 for his second World Cup tournament.

Shop online at
www.mcfc.co.uk

Buying all the latest City kit, training wear and merchandise couldn't be easier with our new online store.

You can purchase items 24 hours a day, 365 days a year.

You can also visit the CityStore at ReebokCity, open seven days a week.

Monday to Saturday - 9am to 5.30pm
Sunday - 11am to 3pm

Exclusive cardholder's discounts available in-store.

Free non-match day parking.

- Shop with confidence, our online service is secure and we do not charge you until we despatch your order.

- Delivery within 5-7 working days, UK orders only.

- Exclusive online only offers on a wide selection of merchandise and souvenirs.

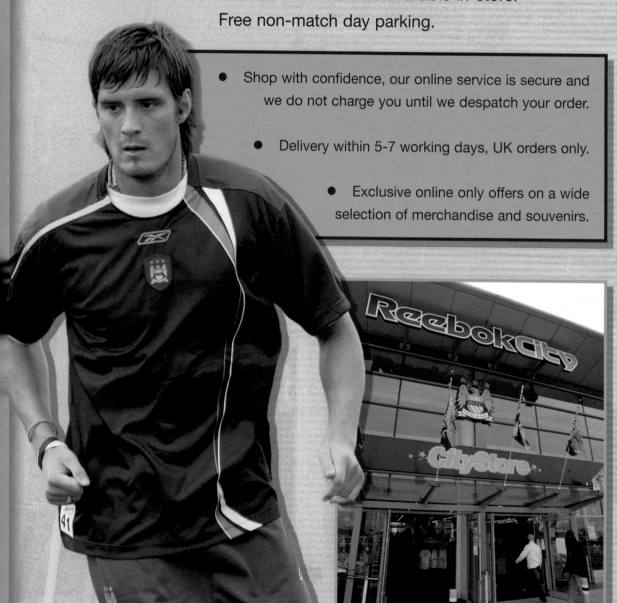

Quiz Answers

Page 19: 2004 - 2005 Quiz

1. David James.
2. Richard Dunne was the first player to be sent off (at Liverpool) and Danny Mills and Christian Negouai also received red cards against Blackburn and Everton respectively.
3. Anelka made his final appearance against Southampton on New Year's Day 2005.
4. Croft made his debut as a substitute against Bolton Wanderers.
5. Bradley Wright-Phillips scored his first goal against Middlesbrough.
6. Ben Thatcher was born in Wiltshire.
7. Lee Croft, Bradley Wright-Phillips and Nedum Onuoha – at England U-20 level.
8. Chelsea, Arsenal and Manchester United all failed to beat City on their own ground.
9. Paul Bosvelt was the oldest at 35 and Nedum Onuoha was aged 17 when he made his debut.
10. Nicolas Anelka (2), Robbie Fowler (2), Antoine Sibierski (1).

Page 26: City Crossword

Page 33: Spot the Ball

Page 33: Silhouettes

Page 46: Moonchester's Guess Who?

1. Willo Flood

2. Danny Mills

3. Robbie Fowler

4. Jonathan D'Laryea